THE FOWLER/MOORE ANCESTRY

A Family History

John L. Moore

Bloomington, IN  Milton Keynes, UK

authorHOUSE®

AuthorHouse™
1663 Liberty Drive, Suite 200
Bloomington, IN 47403
www.authorhouse.com
Phone: 1-800-839-8640

AuthorHouse™ UK Ltd.
500 Avebury Boulevard
Central Milton Keynes, MK9 2BE
www.authorhouse.co.uk
Phone: 08001974150

First published by AuthorHouse   5/2/2007

ISBN: 978-1-4259-7800-6 (sc)

Printed in the United States of America
Bloomington, Indiana

This book is printed on acid-free paper.

DEDICATION

To the woman who put family second only to God in her life, a woman who through strength, determination, and love taught many of us the meaning of "family," and a woman who welcomed me into her family and loved me without reservation. This woman is Viola May (Fowler) Moore, my grandmother.

Viola May Fowler
Circa 1891
Age 4

Material in this book extends from the earliest known ancestors of George Andrew Moore and Viola May Fowler Moore through the end of their lives. The purpose of writing this history is to give George and Viola's descendents an appreciation of who they were, where they came from, and what they experienced as they paved the way for our lives.

This story may be of little interest to those who are not direct descendents or members of the family by marriage. Yet, to those who are, it presents the legacy of our ancestors who literally lived and died so that "the family" could endure. It is not only a story, but a tribute to them.

There are five parts to this history. Part One traces the Fowler side of the family, and Part Two covers the Moore side. Part Three pertains to the time after the two family lines were joined. Part Four gives a family by family summary of George and Viola's children, and Part Five displays our family members in each of the eight generations, beginning with the oldest known ancestor. If you wish to do so, space has been provided at the end to write in the names of new family members who were not born at the time of this writing.

CONTENTS

FORWARD   1

PART ONE: THE FOWLER ANCESTRY   3

PART TWO: THE MOORE ANCESTRY   15

PART THREE: GEORGE ANDREW AND VIOLA MAY   19

PART FOUR: DESCENDENTS OF
    GEORGE ANDREW AND VIOLA MAY MOORE   49

PART FIVE: GENERATIONS OF FOWLER'S
    AND MOORE'S BY BIRTH AND DEATH DATE   55

FORWARD

This story is about family—our family—the Fowlers and the Moores. These two family lines began over eight generations ago and came together in 1903, when George Andrew Moore wed Viola May Fowler. At one time there was a wealth of information about our early ancestors. Viola May could talk for hours about her siblings, her aunts and uncles, and those that preceded them. Unfortunately, little was written down and, though a few stories were passed from generation to generation, much of our family's rich history has been lost. This book is an attempt to capture and record the information we still have before it too fades into antiquity. Thanks to the help of the remaining historical documents and verbal anecdotes, the contents which follow are as historically accurate as possible. That being said, a certain amount of literary license has been taken to fill in gaps, resolve discrepancies in information, and embellish the family history so that the details are richer and more readable.

The Old Home Place
Circa 1927
Photo of the Fowler homestead taken by Henry Schevers long after Will and Malissa Fowler had passed on. All of their children were born in this house, including Viola May, the youngest. Hubert, Roy, and George attended their grandfather's funeral here in January 1921. Their mother, Viola May, could not attend because she had just given birth to her ninth child, Walter.

PART ONE:
THE FOWLER ANCESTRY

Far away from where colonists were rebelling against the British Crown, a baby boy was born. It was circa 1777 when the infant came into the world in a thatched-roof farmhouse in Stoke Saint Millborough, County of Shropshire, nestled in the rich farm country of central England. His parents, whose given names have been lost to antiquity, named him John--John Fowler. It was a name befitting his status as neither an aristocrat nor a peasant. He was born into the agrarian life that characterized that sector of England at the time. Cradled in the Corvs River Valley between the villages of Burwarton and Hopton Cangeford, the fertile fields of Stoke Saint Millborough grew the grain that fed the people of Birmingham and London. Birmingham was a scant thirty miles to the east, although, in the days before the industrial revolution, it had not yet attained the status as a center of industry. At that time, Birmingham was just another sizable town that dotted the English countryside. Though only 120 miles from London, Stoke Saint Millborough was a three-day carriage ride away, over roads that were replete with mud holes, wagon ruts, and bandits. It was indeed a dangerous world into which little John Fowler was born.

According to the Internet source, *Ancestor Search*, Fowler literally means, "A sportsman who pursues wild fowl." It should be no surprise to descendents of the Fowler family that the origin of the name "Fowler" refers to the hunting of wild game, especially fowls. It must have been rooted in their blood because decades of descendents of the oldest known Fowlers have prided themselves as rugged frontiersmen who were skillful with firearms and who provided for their families by hunting wild game.

When he grew up John Fowler could have been a Red Coat fighting for the British in the War of 1812, or he could have been a British seaman on a Man of War rounding the Cape of Good Hope in a treacherous storm, or perhaps a barrister in the Soho District of London. There are no records that reflect he did any of these. More than likely, he grew up and remained on the farm that had been his home in Shropshire County. Census records show that he married Rachel Roberts on April 28, 1803. Though it happened in the same year, the Louisiana Purchase was doubtless of little notice to the young English couple as they began their life in the same simple way as had their parents and their grandparents before them.

Although little is known about John and Rachel Fowler beyond their marriage, census records show that they had at least one child. They named him John Roberts in honor of his father and his father's brother. Ultimately, he would become John Roberts Fowler, Senior.

John Roberts Fowler, Sr., son of John and Rachel, was born in 1805 or 1806 in Stoke Saint Millborough, County of Shropshire, England. He died on November 27, 1897 in Sandusky, Iowa. In his youth, he helped his father to farm the lands that had been in their family for generations. Though he likely never learned to read or write, he profited from his hard labor and became a most eligible bachelor in Shropshire County. In the summer of 1827, John Roberts Fowler married Harriet Hammonds (1808-1837), the daughter of Henry and Ann Hammonds, also of Stoke Saint Millborough.

John Roberts Fowler, Sr.
1806-1897
Circa 1890

During these times, James Madison was president of the United States (1809-1817), and in 1814, Francis Scott Key wrote the Star Spangled Banner. June 18, 1812 was the start of the War of 1812, and in 1815, the upstart Americans fought the British in the Battle of New Orleans. The final tally was U.S. 8 fatalities; the UK 700 dead with another 1200 wounded.

Most of the common folks in England took little notice of the war. This was largely because of the lack of communication. Nevertheless, life went on, and the fledgling Fowler family was typical of England's common folk. Although the ancestry, siblings, and life of John Roberts Fowler, Sr. lacks much in the way of detail, the family of his wife Harriet is well documented. Harriet's parents were Henry and Ann (Bach) Hammonds. They were married on April 16, 1807 at Stanton Lacy. They had four daughters, the oldest of which was Harriet. She was born in 1808 and christened on January 4 of that year. In addition to Harriet, they had Sarah, Mary Ann, and Fanny. Henry Hammonds was a very successful farmer who lived at Hopton Cangeford, in the Parish of Stanton Lacy, Shropshire, England.

In their brief ten years of marriage, John Roberts Fowler, Sr. and Harriet had three sons and no daughters. The sons were William, John Roberts, Jr., and Edwin. In those days christening was held as soon as the infant was old enough to be taken to the church. As a result, William was christened on September 19, 1830 at Hopton Cangeford; John Roberts, Jr. was christened on January 13, 1833 at Stoke Saint Millborough; and Edwin was christened on August 30, 1835 also at Stoke Saint Millborough. Harriet was stricken ill shortly after the birth of her third child and died when Edwin was about eighteen months old (circa 1837). She was only twenty-nine years old.

Three years later, John Roberts, Sr. married Anna Malitt on December 19, 1840 at Stokes Saint Millborough. Anna was born in 1814, also in the vicinity of Shropshire, England. From this marriage came three children, giving the three Fowler boys two half-brothers (James and Herbert Eli) and one half-sister (Emma).

The three sons of Harriet and John Roberts Fowler, along with their father, step-mother, and step-siblings, all immigrated to the United States in 1853. They had heard stories of the new frontier and decided to seek their fortune in this new land of promise and opportunity. At the time, Millard Fillmore was President and California had just been admitted into the union.

Each of the first three sons had inherited a sum of money from the estate of their mother, who, though she was deceased, had received a quarter share from the estate of her parents, Henry and Ann Hammonds. Thus, each of the Fowler brothers received one third of one fourth of the Hammonds' estate. It is curious that Henry and Ann Hammonds died in 1852 and 1854, respectively, but their wills were not fully settled until 1896.

William Fowler (1830-1921), the eldest of the three Fowler brothers, lived to be ninety years old. John Roberts Fowler, Jr. (1833-1897) and Edwin (1835-1921) also lived relatively long lives.

There can be little doubt that hard work and significant challenges characterized the lives of these three brothers. Their mother had died when William, the oldest, was only seven. It was a very early age to assume responsibility for his two younger siblings, but William did so and also helped his father with chores around the house and farm. It should be no surprise, therefore, that the three brothers grew close to one another and, when the opportunity came, they set off together, along with the rest of their family, to seek their fortune in the new land. The three Fowler brothers were only in their teens or early twenties when they boarded the sailing ship in England.

The voyage to the United States took the Fowlers through the port of New Orleans and up the Mississippi River. The Atlantic crossing was made on a sailing vessel called the *Calmalia* which had embarked from England, more than likely from the port at Liverpool. The voyage took more than seven weeks to complete and, when they finally arrived at the mouth of the Mississippi, they found out that they still had an additional riverboat steamer ride of nearly a thousand miles. The steamboat, called the *Alex Scott*, made a profitable business ferrying new arrivals in America from New Orleans to the major cities along the Mississippi River. When they reached St. Louis, Missouri in 1851, they disembarked and spent their first year in America in the city that had become the "Gateway to the West." In 1852, they moved to Keokuk, Iowa, traveling on the steamboat, *Di*

1864
Will Fowler – Age 34
Malissa Fowler – Age 20

Vernon. Some of the family remained in Keokuk, but Will made his way to the village of Montrose, a few miles up the river from Keokuk.

John Roberts, Sr. and several others of the Fowler family eventually settled in Sandusky, Iowa. With few exceptions, the Fowlers determined that their new home should be in Lee County, Iowa. There, they used their savings and inheritance money to purchase farm and timber land and began life in their new country. Much of the land was heavily wooded and had to be cleared, so the work was hard and the profits small. True to their name, the Fowlers relied on their marksmanship and prowess with firearms to provide their families with food. Eventually, each brother separated and went his own way while pioneering the fertile basin that was southeastern Iowa. To the extent that roads and circumstances allowed, they visited each other periodically, but more importantly, even though they had settled miles apart, they remained close in spirit throughout their lives.

1880
Will Fowler – Age 50
Malissa Fowler – Age 36

William applied for U. S. citizenship, but there is no record that he completed the requirements or that he actually became an American citizen. According to family legend, at some point in his early life people stopped calling him William and began calling him Will. So it was documented that Will Fowler married Malissa Bain (1844-1913) in 1860 at Galland, Iowa.

They had eleven children, two of which (both boys) died in infancy. Two other grown sons preceded William in death. Babies born in the late nineteenth century had a life expectancy of less than forty years. By and large, the Fowler's disproved that statistic by living into their eighties and nineties in an era of poor sanitation, rudimentary medical treatment, and hard labor. The seven surviving children who lived exceptionally long lives were: Celestia (Lessie) (1861-1943), Luella (1863-1945), Frank (1873-1963), Hettie (1876-1969), Albert (1879-1968), Arthur (1881-1966), and Viola May (1887-1957).

Will's brother, John Roberts Fowler Jr. purchased a farm near Sandusky upon coming of age and remained there until his death on June 10, 1921. He married Esther Anna McChord in 1860 in Keokuk, and they had six children, four of which were living at his death.. The six were: William J. Fowler, Edward M. Fowler, John C. Fowler, Harriett H. Fowler (Bossler), Ida M. Fowler, and Lillian H. Fowler (Atterberg), all of the Keokuk vicinity.

The youngest brother, Edwin Fowler felt the spirit presented by the new country and decided to see more of it before settling down. For two years during his youth, he drove a tow team for the lighters over the Des Moines River rapids. Although it is now an obsolete business, in the days when navigable waters had rapids and shallows, mule teams were employed to tow the barges and other shallow bottom vessels past the submerged obstacles. After earning enough money to purchase his own team of mules and a wagon, young Edwin headed west for California. He joined a wagon train in Omaha, Nebraska and, just as many other pioneers had done before him, journeyed over the plains and through the Rocky Mountains for many months before arriving in Salt Lake City, Utah. Although he was tempted to remain there, he pressed on and eventually made his way to California in 1861, where he spent the next four years seeking his fortune during the gold rush days in the Sacramento Valley. Just how well Edwin fared is not known, but he did accumulate enough to afford passage on a steamer from San Francisco to New York, traveling around the Cape of Good Hope. He finally returned to Keokuk by taking a train from New York in 1865.

At that time the Civil War had just ended and Abraham Lincoln, our sixteenth President, was about to be assassinated. The country was in turmoil because of the war, the Emancipation Proclamation, and an initiative called "Reconstruction," which had just begun. The citizens of Southern Iowa were still conflicted on the subject of slavery. Most were against it, but some sympathizers lingered on. Few realized how long it would take social attitudes to evolve, but Lincoln understood. He put it in perspective when he said, "Whenever I hear anyone arguing for slavery, I feel a strong impulse to see it tried on him personally."

Edwin Fowler married Emma Haney on April 11, 1875. They produced ten children: Clara Minnie Fowler, George F. Fowler, Ida Fowler, Ella Florence Fowler, Jesse Robert Fowler, William Ernest Fowler, James E. Fowler, Mary Emma Fowler, Minnie Viola Fowler, and Pearl Lucille Fowler. Edwin lived the remainder of his life in Lee County and died on July 20, 1921 at his home in Sandusky. He was survived by four of his ten children: Mrs. Charles Metternich, Mrs. John Boyd, Mr. Jesse R. Fowler, and Mrs. Jesse W. Fruelhling. Ironically, Edwin's half-brother, James, had died a few weeks before. Both had been prominent citizens of Lee County.

Little is known about the three half-siblings of Will, John Roberts, and Edwin after their arrival in America. Emma married twice. Her first marriage was to John Carss on April 5, 1860 and her second was to Asa Z. Parker on October 13, 1896. She died on August 29, 1923 in Keokuk, Iowa. James was known to have journeyed to California, where he lived for a time in Alameda. He returned to Lee County and established a home until his death in 1921. According to some records, he married twice, but little is known about these unions or their children. Eli is also believed to have gone to California, where he supposedly died sometime prior to 1921. Another piece of unconfirmed information is that John Roberts, Sr. and Anna Fowler had a fourth child, a daughter who was delivered, died, and buried at sea during the voyage from England

John Roberts Fowler, Sr., the patriarch of the Fowler clan who had come to America, established themselves, made their fortune, and started more families of Fowlers, ultimately died on November 27, 1897 at age ninety-two. His longevity, along with that of his father, would signal a pattern that characterized the Fowler descendents for generations to come. His obituary in the Daily Gate City newspaper of November 28, 1897 read:

"FOWLER—Near Sandusky, Iowa, Saturday, November 27, 1897,
John Fowler, aged 92 years.

> *The death of John Fowler, an old and highly respected citizen of Lee county occurred at his home near Sandusky yesterday at 7:10 p.m. He was a native of England and came to this country in 1853, locating in Lee county, where he was counted among the early settlers. He was over 91 years of age. For many years he was a resident of Keokuk and removed to Sandusky only two or three years ago. The sympathy of many friends is extended to the surviving family, which includes his sons John and Ed of Sandusky, Will of Montrose, James and Eli and his daughter, Mrs. Parker of Keokuk. His first wife died fifty-eight years ago and his second wife sixteen years ago. The funeral will occur Monday at 2 o'clock from the church in Sandusky."*

The union of John and Rachel had sired three generations of Fowlers and there were more to follow. The descendents of Will and Malissa continued the tradition of living long, yet simple, lives. Most maintained their heritage of staying close to the land, and most of them lived up to their name's origin by hunting in the forests and fields around their homes. They married for life in those days and divorce was unheard of in the Fowler clan. Few ventured very far from Lee County, Iowa, and, in the days when the automobile was a novelty, fewer than half of them drove anything more than a tractor in the field. They had been raised to use animals as beasts of burden and for sustenance when needed. Horses pulled plows, cows gave milk, and chickens produced eggs. Hogs and other livestock were slaughtered on occasion, but the prime source for food on the Fowler table continued to be from the hunting of wildlife that was abundant on their land.

The direct descendents of Will and Malissa Fowler were:

Lessie, the eldest, married Terpin Slater (1852-1918). From that marriage, two children were born. Their son, Walter Slater (1890-1967) married Iva Ball (1894-1993). Lessie and Terpin's daughter, Lula (1885-1951) married William Swinderman (1882-1967). They produced two children, Wilber (-) and Garnett (Klingner) (-).

Luella married William Smith (1864-1901). They had a daughter, Lessie (1888-1982) who married Frank Hopp (1884-1970). They had four children. Hazel (Herschler) (-), Frank Jr. (-), Erith (-), and Nedra (Benjamin) (-).

George William married Elizabeth Brumagen (1870-1946).

Frank and Clara Fowler
Circa 1900

John W. Married Elizabeth Findeis (-1910).

James E. (1870-1874) died early.

Frank, the sixth oldest of William and Mallissa's children married Clara Hagan (1880-1970). They had six children: Earl, Mabel (Finerty), George, Mildred (Deer), Marie (Lane) and Edna (Bensinger).

The next oldest was Mary Hettie, who was called Hettie. She married Henry Schevers (1876-1949). They had one adopted daughter, Francis (1926-2000) who married Frances Showalter (1922-1995).

Albert married Dora Sullivan (1880-1943), and they had five children. Long after Dora died, Albert remained on the old home place. It became, not only the place the Fowlers remembered as "home," it was gathering place for family reunions and for hunting. Acres of timber and corn fields were full of squirrels, rabbits, raccoons, quails, pheasants, and turkeys. The Fowlers and their descendents spent many hours scouring the rolling terrain for wild game. Rarely did they return empty-handed.

The eldest of Albert and Dora's children, Elma (1904-2001) married Jess Frueling (1886-1991). Elma and Jess had eight children. Ivor (-) and his wife Dorothy live in Roselle, IL. Craig (-) and his wife Jeannie live in Middlefield, OH. Delmar (-) and his wife, Karlene live in Romeoville, IL. Donald (-) and his wife, Gudrun live in Potomac, MD. Vernon (-) and his wife, Denise live in St. Louis, MO. Merline (-) lives in Redwood City, CA. Lois (-), and her husband Walter Sheffler live in Blythe, CA. Dolores (-) lives in Marshfield, MO.

The second child of Albert and Dora was William (1902-1978). He never married.

Hazel (1907-1961), the third to be born, married Irvin Anderson (1902-1986).

Their fourth child, Helen (1908-1992) married Glenn Welden (1897-1967).

Wilma (1914-2002), the youngest, married James Harmon (1915-1985). They had a daughter, Gloria (-).

Arthur married Gertie Dugan (1882-1952). They had three children. Hilda (1906-1937) married Allie Brisby (1901-1939). Lloyd (1912-1968) married Ruby Stockwell (1916-2001). Bernice (1914-2003) married Glen Petty (1913-1993).

Hettie and Henry Schevers
1895

Arthur and Gerta Fowler
Circa 1903

Charles died in infancy on March 13, 1884.

The youngest of the children of Will and Malissa Fowler was Viola May (1887-1957). She married George Moore (1882-1973) and produced ten children. Their life and the story of their descendents are told in subsequent sections.

The original Fowler traditions and heritage have not been lost in the succeeding generations. Longevity is a Fowler trademark, with each generation producing at least one nonagenarian. The oldest thus far is believed to be Hubert A. Moore who lived to be nearly ninety six years old.

The tendency to live off the land has diminished somewhat, as modern day civilization encourages urbanization. Nonetheless, hunting and fishing remain a prominent part of many of the Fowler descendents' lives, though now as a sport rather than a source of food.

Viola May and George Andrew Moore
Wedding Day
1903

Fowler Family
Circa 1889
Bluff Park, Montrose, Iowa
(The little girl in the white dress marked with an "x" is Viola May)

It is doubtful that John and Rachel could have imagined what would happen. Eight generations of Fowlers have emerged from those early days in Shropshire. The descendents of John and Rachel total in the hundreds, if not thousands, but it is not the number that is significant. The real importance of their legacy is that they charted a life that was honest, hard-working, and God-fearing. Their children passed it on to their children, and, from generation to generation, the heritage spread. Today, a baby born to a descendent of John Fowler has no concept of what preceded him, yet the Fowler blood is in his veins. He will thrive and continue the traditions of longevity, dedication to family, and respect for God.

PART TWO:
THE MOORE ANCESTRY

The earliest identified ancestor on the Moore side of the family was David Moore, who, according to handwritten records, was born on December 1, 1764 somewhere on the East Coast. His Fowler contemporary in England, John Fowler, would not be born for thirteen more years. Little is known about David Moore except that he married Lucretia Davis, who was born on August 31, 1763. One can speculate about their origins and later life, but, as these were times prior to the American Revolutionary War, their place of birth, childhood, and marriage time and location would be just that–speculation. However, we know that they eventually migrated to what was then known as the Territory of Kentucky, where they settled to raise their family.

While John Fowler was growing up in Shropshire England, David and Lucretia Moore gave birth to a son who they named George C. Little George was born on the American frontier in what is now Lincoln County, Kentucky. This wilderness territory had not yet been admitted into the union, and, scarcely two decades had passed since the original thirteen colonies had become the original thirteen states. The struggle of the American nation and its people involved wagon trains probing the frontier, settlements carved from virgin forests, and hardships we can scarcely imagine today. Sometime in 1820, the marriage of George C. to Rhoda Elmore (12/3/1793-2/14/1868) became one of the earliest recorded events in the Moore family history. In that year, James Monroe was the country's President and the United States was pursuing such notable achievements as purchasing Florida from Spain, building the Cumberland Road, and issuing the Monroe Doctrine, which announced to the world that this new nation was one to be reckoned with.

Andrew Jackson had just been elected President when Rhoda presented George C with their fourth child, a son who they named Shapley. The history of Lee County, Iowa records a number of events pertaining to the Moores, among them that young Shapley (pronounced with a short "a" as in snap) Moore was born on May 10, 1829 in Lincoln County, Kentucky.

Shapley was seven years old when his parents moved the family from Kentucky to the Iowa Territory. In June of 1836, they settled in Charleston Township of Lee County where they purchased a homestead consisting of one hundred and twenty acres of land, eighty of which were in good, tillable condition. George C. and Rhoda would become the parents of nine children--four sons and five daughters. They were among the earliest settlers in the region and, despite having to endure difficulties of a pioneer life, they set the example for the many who followed. These two early founders of the Moore clan remained at their Charleston farm for the remainder of their days, at which time the farm was sold.

Shapley lived under his parent's roof until he was twenty-three years old. In 1852, he joined two of his good friends, Dietrick Felcher and Roy Gilliam, seeking their fortune in the gold rush frenzy of California. They embarked on a sailing vessel from New Orleans via the Nicaragua route, eventually docking in San Francisco. After passing under the Golden Gate Bridge, Shapley made his way to the gold mines of the Sacramento and Feather River Valleys. There, he spent the next two decades of his life digging for the yellow ore.

Shapley found financial success in California, but he was homesick for friends and family in Iowa. In the early 1870's, he returned to Lee County, where he found his boyhood farm was no longer in the family. He used his

Shapley Moore (Circa 1865)

mining earnings to repurchase the homestead his father had established some four decades earlier. For the first time in years, it was a period of peace across the nation. Reconstruction had ended, and the South was forging a new economy without slavery. In a bold move in 1867, during the Andrew Johnson administration, Secretary of State William Seward purchased the territory of Alaska for what most people thought was an exorbitant price— two cents an acre. They called it Seward's Folly.

On November 5, 1871, in Galand, Iowa and at the mature age of 42, Shapley married a young widow.

Only thirty years old, the widow, Mrs. Melvina Fickle, was the daughter of George and Katie Hiler. Originally from Ohio, in 1858 the Hilers came to Charleston Township, where they settled and raised nine children, of which Melvina was the oldest. She was born in Brown County, Ohio on January 5, 1841 and, as a young lady, married William Fickle, who died in Charleston on June 28, 1867. Though barely twenty-six years old at the time of his death, Melvina had already bore four children. Their names were Frank, Minnie, Chris W., and Clara. Melvina and Shapley raised her four plus they were blessed with two of their own, Lula and George Andrew.

Elsewhere during that time, Ulysses S. Grant served as President, the transcontinental railroad was completed at Promontory Point, Utah, and General Custer was massacred at the battle of Little Bighorn.

Despite their late start in marriage, Shapley and Melvina were quite successful. The farm originally purchased and homesteaded by George C. and Rhoda was once again in the Moore family. Shapley and Melvina continued to work to make their home one of the finest in the county. In addition to the rich Iowa soil in the fields, the farm consisted of a comfortable, frame dwelling, a good barn and out-buildings, plus everything needed to be a first class farm estate. Between the earnings in the gold fields and the profits from the farm, the Shapley Moores had become one of the more affluent families of the area. Their home displayed all of the comforts and many of the luxuries available to Americans in the late eighteen hundreds.

To be financially comfortable in those days was a rarity. One of the drawbacks of life for the early settlers was the scarcity of money. Bartering was more common than actual cash payment for most goods and services. At the time, postage on letters was twenty-five cents, which was collected from the recipient. Frequently, they would have to let letters from friends remain weeks in the post office for the want of a quarter. Lending institutions such as banks were able to charge fifty percent interest because of the scarcity of money.

Melvina Hiler Fickle Moore
Circa 1881

The Lee County History reports that both Shapley and Melvina were connected with the Baptist church and that, politically, Shapley was a staunch Republican. They enjoyed a marked degree of esteem and the friendship of a large circle of friends. Both Shapley and Melvina spent the later years of their lives enjoying the fruits of their early industry.

These years saw the Statue of Liberty erected on Ellis Island, the great Chicago World's Fair, and electricity placed in the White House.

Shapley died in 1895, but Melvina lived on and remarried a third husband whose name was Westfall. Melvina died in 1913 at the age of seventy-four, but was remembered by her grandchildren for her kindness and visits. They called her Grandma Westfall.

One of Shapley's sisters, Leann Moore, married a man named Cox. Another sister, Lucretia Moore, married Samuel Pickard in 1843. The accounts of Mr. Pickard in the Lee County History are of interest as they provide a glimpse into the lifestyle of the time. After coming to Lee County in 1839, Samuel Pickard landed his first job. It was called "breaking prairie" and involved driving a team of oxen pulling a wooden plow from sun up to sun down. Coming from the fertile and previously tilled fields of Indiana, he found prairie breaking in Southeast Iowa to be much more difficult. At the time he lived in Cedar Township with never more than six other families. He assisted in constructing the first schoolhouse, which was built of round 16" x 18" logs, heated by an open-hearth fireplace, and topped off with a chimney made of sticks and clay.

When given the opportunity, he jumped at the chance to change from "ox driver" to "school teacher." However, soon after he began the first term, he contracted an ailment they called "AUGE." The origin of the term "AUGE" has been lost over the centuries and it was probably slang for something else. Nevertheless, AUGE was a malady caused by inhaling decaying prairie sod and vegetation. It apparently came from breathing air loaded with extremely vile effluvium, and it caused the patient to tremble uncontrollably. In those days, AUGE was described as a "chief torment." A friend writing to Samuel in the fall of 1840 wished to know if they had much AUGE. Samuel replied "It is here in most abundance. Everyone has it. As to its severity, why bless you, you can have no idea. It can't be described. A quarrelsome wife is no comparison to it. It shakes all creation out here." In addition to being a farmer and school teacher, Samuel Pickard joined the Missionary Baptist Church and became a licensed preacher. One of the county's first circuit riders, he traveled to destitute neighborhoods, preaching the gospel to folks who otherwise had no place to go to church.

Lula and George Andrew profited from the comparatively comfortable and easy-going lifestyle of the farm in Charleston, but neither wanted to continue farming when they were grown. Lula married John Reuther and lived in Lee County for the rest of her life.

Shapley and Melvina had done well. All six children were raised and out of the home before Shapley died. As the only male heir in the Moore lineage, the responsibility to continue the family name fell squarely on the shoulders of George Andrew. History would show that he was up to the challenge.

PART THREE:
GEORGE ANDREW AND VIOLA MAY

George Andrew found work with the railroad and began a life of hard labor in hard times, yet with rich rewards after marrying Viola May Fowler in 1903. Their first child, Roy, was born in 1905. A second child, who they named Lloyd, was born in the dead of winter in 1908. He lived for only three days. They had no idea that, of the eight children to come later, all but one would be boys. In 1904-1906, Theodore Roosevelt was President, the U.S. obtained rights to the Panama Canal, and San Francisco suffered the most devastating earthquake in its history.

Hubert at age two

George Andrew worked for the Chicago, Burlington, and Quincy (CB&Q) Railroad as a member of what was called the "section gang." It was so named because they were in charge of maintaining a specific section of track for the railroad.

In the days before automobiles, most laborers walked to work. Therefore, they needed to live close to the railroad section to which they were assigned. One of the first sections which George Andrew worked on was in Argyle, Iowa, which is where he and Viola married. Some time later, they moved to Mount Hamil, Iowa, again to be in the town closest to the stretch of track of his new assignment. It was there that their third child, Hubert Arthur, was born.

As the years passed, more births occurred, and the Moore family multiplied. After Hubert, there was George Raymond in 1911. Then came the twins, Chester and Lester, in 1914, followed closely by Harold in 1915. Three boys within fifteen months of age gave Viola extra wrinkles and gray hair. The boys' only sister, Velma Alberta, was born on a cold November day in 1918. She lived only seven days and her passing was one of the most difficult ordeals Viola had to endure, and it haunted her for the rest of her life. Two more boy babies would complete the family. Walter was born in 1921 and Milton came along in 1924.

The fledgling Moore family moved to Fort Madison, Iowa in about 1912 and rented a small wood-frame house in the 1400 block of Avenue G, but it was then called Second Street. Those were the days of no public electricity, water, or sewer, unpaved streets, and, although the automobile had been around for a few years, transportation was mainly by foot or by horseback. On the corner to the east of their home was Callie Scholtz's blacksmith shop, where Mr. Scholtz shoed the horses that were the primary means of transportation for both people and goods. The little Moore boys found great entertainment in watching Mr. Scholz nail horseshoes to the horse's hooves.

The world was on the brink of World War I. The United States sought to remain neutral, but the sinking of the Lusitania, among other reasons, caused Congress to declare war on Germany in 1917. By 1919, the "war to end all wars" had ended and the country settled into a new era. The Prohibition Amendment was passed in 1919 outlawing alcohol, and the next year, the nineteenth amendment, giving women the right to vote, became law.

Moore Family at 1312 Des Moines Street

Front Row: George Andrew, Harold, Roy, Frank Fowler, Ralph Johns, Chester, Lester, Marie Fowler, Mildred Fowler, and George Raymond

Back Row: Hubert, Hettie Fowler Schevers, Mrs. Johns and son, Clara Fowler, Viola, and Walter

Life was simple in those days. People were far more self-reliant than they are today for their basic needs. Still, there were stores, taverns, and even a pool hall in their neighborhood. What folks couldn't grow in their garden, they bought from Able's Grocery Store, where they ran a monthly bill. Back then, that was the modern equivalent of a credit card. The main difference between the two is that there were no bank guarantees and only the good name of the shopper gave the grocer any assurance that he would be paid when the shopper's paycheck came at the end of the month. George and Viola Moore made ends meet, and, despite a meager paycheck, they always paid something on their bill. It was a matter of pride, and they taught that lesson to their children.

The Fort Madison of the early nineteen hundreds was a sprawling community running several miles along the Mississippi River. Unlike many other towns its size, it sported a street car system. As the town was long and narrow, street cars were an efficient means to transport people from the west end of town to the business district located at the eastern border. The street car ran from the end of Fourth Street past the Federal Penitentiary through the residential area and ended at the Perfection Tire Company in the far western edge of town. Cobblestones were laid to separate and hold the steel rails of the street car tracks in place. Years later, when the street car system was discontinued, the bumpy cobblestone streets remained to serve the automobile traffic. They constituted a rough roadway, but they were an improvement over the dirt wagon paths they replaced.

George and Hubert Moore, Bernice and Lloyd Fowler, Circa 1920

Fort Madison was a river town that was established as a way station for barge and steamboat traffic moving up and down the Mississippi. It also provided the right-of-way for railroads that crisscrossed the nation at the start of the century. The CB&Q and the Santa Fe railroads were prominent in the town and provided jobs to young men who were willing to shovel coal for the steam-powered locomotives. Later, when diesel-powered engines replaced the steam locomotives, railroad firemen either learned to operate the diesels or they found other work because their jobs had become obsolete.

Near the end of the War, the Moore's bought their first house at 1312 Des Moines Street, later called Avenue I. It was not modern in any way, but it did have a holding tank and pump in the cellar from which cistern water was pumped by pressure up to a tank in the kitchen. The cistern water was used only for dishwashing, laundry, and cleaning. For drinking water, there was a well just outside the back door. Summer or winter, the well had to be kept primed for it was the only source of potable water. In the winter, they had to thaw out the pump in order to make it work. In a strange rite of passage, each Moore boy took his turn placing his tongue on the frozen pump handle to see if it really would stick. It did. Usually, once was enough, but Viola used to laugh that it took George Raymond a couple of times to learn that lesson. Also, the pump that served the cistern had to be operated quite often or it would lose its prime and the Moore boys would not be able to bathe. Pumps in those days were strictly manual, and they weren't overly reliable.

Since there was no city water, and pumps and cisterns were the only source of water for everyone, the man who could repair pumps and dig wells held a position of eminence. Mr. Brandenberger, who lived on Avenue H, was the pump and well repairman.

George, Viola, and their five boys lived in that small, austere house for about eleven years. Roy and Hubert slept in one bed in the front bedroom. In the living room, there was a Duofold couch that had to be made up into a bed every night. That's where the twins, Chester and Lester, as well as George slept. However, their family would continue to expand, so it wasn't long before they totally out-grew the two bedrooms, living room, and kitchen of 1312 Des Moines Street.

By the start of the second decade of the twentieth century, the George A. Moore family had grown to seven boys. George A. had established himself as knowledgeable section hand and had shown signs of leadership. Soon, the railroad would make him a section foreman. In 1924, the last of the children of George and Viola was born. Another boy, Milton Earl, would become the first, and only one, of their sons to graduate from college.

Technology began to progress rapidly in the years following World War I. Warner Brothers produced the first talking movie, John Baird invented the first television, and, in 1927, Charles Lindbergh flew across the Atlantic. Yet, the 1920's were also days before electric refrigerators were available or affordable. Ice was delivered every day from either Benbow or Weisner Ice Companies. Everyone had an "ice box," and ice delivery was a big business. In winter, ice was cut from the river, brought to large icehouses, and covered with sawdust to keep it from thawing. Amazingly, the large concentration of ice could be kept solid long into the summer. In later years, the ice companies used an ammonia refrigeration system to make the ice. There were very few trucks and the ice was delivered on horse-drawn ice wagons. It was always a treat for the Moore boys to jump on the back of the ice wagon and ride toward school. After a few years, the Artesian Ice Company took over for Benbow and Weisner and continued to make and deliver ice right up to the start of World War II. It was then that the first refrigerators became affordable for low income people such as George and Viola Moore. It was tiny by today's standards and had a freezer only big enough to freeze a couple of dozen ice cubes. Even after she had her first electric refrigerator, Viola kept the old icebox out on the porch for a long time. Perhaps she thought that the electric refrigerator might only be a passing fad.

In about 1928, they moved to 1916 Avenue I, where the Moore family, which now numbered ten, could spread out in *four* bedrooms. That was to become George and Viola's permanent homestead: where they toiled, laughed, and prayed, where they completed the task of raising their eight boys, and where they would come to their final rest some five decades later.

Not only did the house at 1916 Avenue I not have running water or indoor toilets when they first moved in, it also had no electricity. They read and ate by a coal oil lamp with a

1916 Avenue I
Fort Madison, Iowa

Viola May and George Andrew Moore
1920

reflector behind it. The first electric lights that replaced the old gas and kerosene lamps consisted of a light bulb dangling from a single cord in the middle of each room, operated by a pull chain.

Heat came from a potbelly stove located in the dining room and a cook stove in the kitchen. As the stove had a reservoir for hot water, it heated water for both cleaning and cooking. It was also where the Moore boys lined up for their Saturday night bath. Next to the stove was a large wooden washtub. Water heated on the cook stove was poured into the tub, and everyone took their turns, beginning with the oldest. Viola used to say, "Stick the top of your body out and wash as far down as possible. Then, stick your bottom out and wash as far up as possible. Then, wash possible."

Christmas was not very lavish for the Moore family of the 1920's. Santa Claus brought his usual little pile of overalls, shirts, and socks for each of the boys but much of what they received were hand-me-downs. One year they were all collectively given a farm wagon. The enterprising boys took it to the neighbors and asked to haul their trashcans of ashes, etc. to the Doty dump located about three blocks south of the house. It was not unusual to work all day for seventy-five cents.

Viola May's nickname was "Carrie." It was a nickname given to her because of her intense hatred of drinking and gambling. "Carrie Nation" was the turn-of-the-century woman who became famous for using her hatchet to chop up booze joints wherever she found them. George A. and all of her brothers called her Carrie, but it was with great affection. It is interesting to note that in 1933, during the Franklin Roosevelt administration, Prohibition was repealed.

George Andrew was also known as a man with an intense dislike for pool playing. He frequently admonished his sons by saying that if he ever caught them inside Enderlie's Pool

Hall, he'd take the belt to them. No one knew for certain why he felt so strongly, but it was rumored that, as a young lad, he had been given a costly lesson in pool playing by some traveling hustler.

George and Viola gave up virtually all outside pleasures so their children could have just a little more. However, their attendance at once-a-month church dinners was an exception. It was a custom in the First Christian Church of Fort Madison to host a family night at which everyone brought baskets of food and ate together in pot luck fashion. There was always a little program put on by someone involving music or a skit, and, of course, they would sing hymns. Viola had her favorites, and all the boys knew the words to "The Old Rugged Cross" by heart.

They had no car, so the two-mile trip to and from the church was made on foot every Sunday. Even though they lived hand-to-mouth, they always found something to

*Viola and George Moore going
to church (Circa 1925)*

put in the church envelope each week. Like most churches of the early twentieth century, the pews were rock hard, the sermons were long, and air conditioning was unknown. George and Viola would line their brood up in one pew which others called "the Moore pew". It was George's job to look each boy over, and, once in awhile, bring out his handkerchief, wet it with his tongue, and clean out any dirt, real or imagined, from the boys' ears.

George and Viola both worked from early morning to late night. It was necessary for survival. George would fill the old copper boiler with water just before bed time so it could heat up all night on the cook stove in the kitchen. He would get up around four a.m. and run the clothes through the first wash. Later, the older boys would run the hand machine used for the second wash and then run the clothes through the first and second rinses. It was a very labor-intensive and time-consuming process. One time, Roy was using the hand wringer to wring out the clothes. The cogs fascinated Hubert, who everyone thought was mechanically inclined. As if to disprove their conviction, Hubert stuck his finger in the cogs, and the wringer grabbed it. Before Roy could stop, Hubert's index finger had gone through. By good fortune, the finger was not severed, but there was a ting of blood in the wash water that week, and Hubert wore a lasting scar for years afterward. When the washing was done and Hubert's bleeding had stopped, the water had to be hand carried outside and placed on Viola's flower beds. All told, it was a laborious process.

Speaking of laborious processes, George would half-sole all of their shoes. He had all the different "shoe templates" to fit the shoe for each boy. From flat pieces of tanned leather, he would cut the sole according to the pattern and stitch the resulting half-sole to the bottom of the shoe.

Chester and Lloyd
1944

Viola had a foot-treadle sewing machine, and she would sew late into the night, making underwear out of sugar and flour sacks. Viola's talent on the sewing machine extended beyond underwear, as she could make shirts and other garments as well. She also collected old rags from clothing and other items and wove them into throw rugs. Anyone who awakened late at night could hear her sewing away.

Amid all the hardships and endless work, the Moore family also experienced times of great sadness. One chilly autumn day in 1928, Chester, who was called Chet, and two other classmates decided to skip school and go out on the Mississippi River to hunt ducks. All the boys had been warned about the dangers out on the mighty Mississippi, but the confidence of youth overcame those warnings. Chet was a high school sophomore at the time. A storm came up, and the wind blew from the north so hard that they were struggling mightily to row back to shore. In fact, the rowing was so strenuous that they raised blisters on their hands. To combat the exhaustion and the blisters, the boys took turns at the oars which required them to frequently exchange places in the boat. On one such exchange, a classmate slipped, and his shotgun went off. Chet was shot in the leg just below the knee. Somehow, they managed to overcome the wind and the current and, in a boat filled with terror, made it to shore. They were fortunate that they didn't all drown as the boat was swamped with icy water and Chet's blood. After a day or two in the hospital, infection set in and the doctors had to remove Chet's leg just above the knee.

The 1920's continued to bring grief. The country had just come out of World War I and the times known as the Roaring Twenties, when along came the Great Depression. The stock market crash of May, 1929 would begin a period of severe national distress, yet also a period when its citizens were able to show their true mettle. A family that had been struggling in the so-called "good" times, was now faced with even greater economic challenges. Of some consolation, George A. remained employed. The railroads were one of the few industries that survived the depression years with some dignity. Nevertheless, things simply weren't available. The interdependent economic forces of goods, services, capital, and trade all seemed to grind to a halt. No one had any money to buy anything, but it didn't make any difference because there was nothing to buy. If they hadn't learned anything else, the Moore family knew the meaning of thrift. One day, when Harold was in the yard eating a sandwich, he threw a piece of the bread crust on the ground. Viola made him get it and feed it to the chickens. She scolded him, "In this family, we don't waste anything." It was a lesson that carried them all through the depression and for the rest of their lives.

George Andrew in 1948

The housewife of the early twentieth century made meals from scratch, and Viola was no exception. She baked all of the family's bread, pies, cakes, cookies, and especially homemade cinnamon rolls. She was an excellent cook and could prepare a tasty meal from almost anything. Made from an old soup bone, a few left over vegetables, and a loving touch, her vegetable soup with homemade noodles was a work of art.

After working all day, George would come home and tend to his garden, which grew most of the food for the family table. His plot of ground was not large enough for all of the crops, so he would rent other lots for potatoes, corn, etc. After the harvest, everyone pitched in to prepare the produce for canning. They also picked cherries, strawberries, and apples "on the share". The orchards got half, and the Moores got half. Most of these orchards were along the tracks, so George would take two or three boys on the railroad handcar. No one even thought about liability in those times.

They had a dirt-floor fruit cellar in the basement where potatoes and other canned goods were stored. A big stone crock, holding ten or fifteen gallons of sour kraut, was also placed in the basement. Quite often in those hard times, hoboes from the rail yard would come up the alley and knock on their back door, asking for something to eat. Not once did Viola turn them away. She would make them eggs and potatoes and occasionally accept some work in return. When asked why she always fed them all, she said, "Never turn a person away who is hungry." It was her amendment to the Golden Rule. The word must have gotten out to the hoboes because, in forty years, she never had one of them turn on her.

George and Viola kept chickens in an old tarpaper-sided barn next to the alley. The chickens were the source of the two fried eggs that George had every morning before he walked two miles to work. Every Saturday night, they selected one of the chickens to be a guest at Sunday dinner the next day. The chopping block that stood ominously next to the chicken yard gate and the sharpened hatchet were essential tools in an era where people fended for themselves. George was in charge of the chopping and Viola did the cooking.

At work, George kept a gunnysack with him and, when he left the depot where he got his company mail, he picked up chunks of coal that had dropped off the coal cars. Every day, he lugged the heavy sack back to his tool house. When he got a bin full, he wheeled a wheelbarrow in to work and brought home the coal. Another source of fuel also came from the railroad. Old railroad ties, taken out from under the rails when they were replaced with new ones, were hauled to 1916 Avenue I by Mr. Baxter, a friend who had a horse and wagon. The ties were sawed into chunks for the heating stove or chopped into smaller pieces for the cook stove.

In addition to being hard-working, patriotic, and honest, George and Viola were religious and righteous people. In later years, after most of her children were married, Viola took a job teaching the "ladies' bible class" at the church. One of the fondest memories of any who knew her was when she would sit at the dining room table reading her favorite bible passages after all the work was done and her family was in bed. She advocated doing good because it is good. She studied the Book of Revelations and often proclaimed that the next world war would start in the holy land, and the next time God would destroy the earth, it would be by fire.

All of the Moore boys had chores to do, and George and Viola saw that they were done. At Christmas time, George A. and the older boys would go out in the country and chop down cedar trees. They kept the best one for their front room yuletide decoration and sold the rest. One-half of their profits always went to Viola to help pay the bills.

The advent of social security in 1935 would protect the working man by giving him a pension after his laboring years were done. All of these programs were hailed as magnificent by George and Viola, and their loyalty to Franklin Delano Roosevelt and the Democratic Party was solidified. FDR's "new deal" was just beginning to have its effect. Programs such as the CCC, NRA, and TVA were bringing the nation back to work.

As the nation struggled to emerge from the Great Depression in the mid-nineteen thirties, the Moore family continued their struggle for survival. The older boys, Roy and Hubert, found work, left home, and married. George Raymond followed in his father's footsteps and worked for the railroad, first as a fireman and later as an engineer. Lester, Chester, and Harold went to work at the Sheaffer Pen Company, the primary manufacturer in Fort Madison. Walter became a butcher, and Milton was still at home, and so it appeared that life was settling down for the Moore family in the early thirties. However, nothing devastated the family more than what happened on May 3, 1935.

It was early 1935 when Roy and his wife Leona moved close to Monmouth, Illinois because he was assigned to the Ormonde oil pipeline pumping station. Roy was always fond of hunting and firearms. One night, he was cleaning his rifle

Roy Moore, 1925

29

since he was planning to go down to their Uncle Albert's farm to hunt squirrels. With only one shell in the chamber, the gun accidentally went off, and the bullet pierced his heart. Leona was away playing cards with some lady friends at the time. When she came home and found him, he was dead. His daughters, Carol June and LaVonne, were still in bed asleep.

Leona called her priest, and the priest called George and Viola, saying "You had better come. There has been a terrible accident."

Viola, George and grandson, Larry, 1936

Harold (Rosy) Moore
1932

They called Hubert, who was then working for the pipeline at East Fort Madison and had a car. They made the trip to Monmouth not knowing Roy was dead until they arrived at midnight. His funeral was held at Fort Madison, and he was buried at Sacred Heart Cemetery.

Leona later moved back to Fort Madison, where she and her two young daughters lived, until several years later when she married Russell Soland, a farmer from Nauvoo, Illinois. Although quite a bit older than Leona, he was a good husband and stepfather to Roy's girls. It was one of the hardest things the family had faced in life, and Viola, in particular, never got over it.

The remainder of the nineteen thirties was happier. The depression was easing a bit. The Moore boys were star athletes in high school, particularly at football. Lester came along first

Milton and John 1942

Hubert Moore at Williamsburg, VA, 1944

and was an elusive halfback for the Fort Madison Bloodhounds. Not to be outdone, Harold also played halfback and was named All State his senior year.

Soon, Milton carried on the tradition, starring in football and track. He continued to play in college, becoming the first of the Moore clan to, not only attend, but also play intercollegiate football at Culver Stockton College in Canton, Missouri.

The boys graduated, marriages took place, and grandchildren were born--all in the thirties, but no one could imagine what the forties would bring to the Moore family. The attack on December 7, 1941 was truly a day in infamy, and it brought a resounding impact to the Moores, along with the entire nation.

Four of the seven Moore brothers were called into service. Hubert joined the Navy as a machinist mate, serving at Great Lakes Naval Station, Illinois. Though he never saw overseas duty, he was on the verge of shipping out to the Pacific Theater when the war ended.

Harold, who was also known as Rosy because of his rosy cheeks, spent over four years in the Army and participated in fierce battles in France, Belgium, and Germany.

These were tough times for everyone, but particularly for families with loved ones in combat. While the four Moore boys were serving their country, Germany and her Axis allies had captured most of Europe, and Japan had gained control of much of the Pacific Theater. Every American knew the country was at war and they pulled together in the fight.

Things at home were different than anyone had ever seen them. The country was in an all out campaign

Harold (Rosy) and Dorothy at the Fort Madison Depot at the end of a furlough

to win the war and bring the boys home. Rationing was in place, and materials needed for the war effort were hard to come by. Ration stamps were parceled out to buy many necessities, but Americans found that they could get by with less. They planted victory gardens to grow food. They saved rags, newspapers, and scrap iron for the war. Women left their homes, rolled up their sleeves, and stood toe to toe with the men on the assembly lines making tanks, bullets, and uniforms. Dorothy worked at the shell plant, an armaments company in Burlington, and other Moore sister-in-laws pitched in to aid the cause. There was no metal for toys, so Hubert made an army truck out of wood for his son, John. Rubber and gasoline were scarce, so everyone walked and left their cars in the garage. With the few extra pennies they had, people bought war bonds. They gave blood and sent boxes of cookies to the troops overseas. It was a magnificent effort and reflected the stuff of which the Moores and other Americans were made.

The third Moore to be inducted in the Army was Walter, who served in the Pacific.

George, Viola, Walter, Louise and Barbara Ann Moore in 1943

The youngest brother, Milton, enlisted in the Army at age nineteen and fought in campaigns both in Europe and in the Aleutians.

One of Viola's fondest anecdotes was about how she knew where Milton was going to be stationed, even though troop movements were kept at the highest level of secrecy. Before he shipped out, he wrote her a letter nearly every day. One day, she announced to the family that she knew where he was going. "Where?" they asked. "Dutch Harbor, in the Aleutian Islands," was her reply. How did she know? "From the letters," she said.

Everyone read the letters many times, pouring over them, trying to detect what code Milton had used. No one found it. Finally, she revealed how she knew. The first letter was addressed to Mrs. George D. Moore; the second to Mrs. George U. Moore, etc. No one but her thought to read the addresses, and the dozen or so letters spelled out where her baby boy was going. A mother's intuition perhaps, but she knew he would find a way to tell her.

One day, on the outskirts of a small German village, the 113th Mechanized Calvary was moving up to protect the flank of Milton's outfit, the 86th Infantry Division. The infantry division had gone several days without supplies, including meals. On that particular day,

George and Milton in 1944

the unit had received some badly needed C-rations, and Milton was sitting on a stone wall next to a farmhouse, preparing to eat. Oblivious of the fact that he was sitting on the wall of a manure pen, he was devouring the C-rations when a jeep drove by. Thinking it might be a high ranking officer, he looked up. Milt thought the jeep passenger looked familiar, and bore a close resemblance to his brother Rosy. Taking a chance, Milton yelled out Rosy's name and the jeep stopped. As unlikely as it was, there were the two brothers who hadn't seen each other since the war began and who had no idea the other was in Germany, locked in a bear hug. Viola told the story over and over again, firmly convinced that their meeting was the result of her prayers.

Each day between 1941 and V.J. Day in 1945 was a torture for Viola and George. They celebrated the end of the war and the return of all four sons by continuing to live their lives in a simple, uncomplicated, yet God-fearing way. With the war over, their sons at home, and the economy booming, it seemed like life was finally smoothing out for George and Viola. However, it wasn't quite that easy.

In the fall of 1945, Hubert and his wife Helen divorced. Their son John was awarded to Hubert, but that was a problem as well as a blessing. Hubert had just been discharged from the Navy, had not resettled into his job, and couldn't work and mind a five-year-old at the same time. That's when Viola and George stepped in and offered to house, cook, and care for both Hubert and John at their home at 1916 Avenue I. No timetable was given; the offer was good for as long as it took. So, after raising eight boys to adulthood, Viola, at age fifty-eight, took on her ninth "son."

Milton, Viola May, Harold, and John
1948

John and Hubert stayed at the Avenue I home for over five years, during which John learned the same lessons that had been taught to his uncles a few decades earlier. During that time, Harold returned home for a short time after the war, as did Milton before going to college.

Even though they had left the nest, 1916 Avenue I was still home to her boys, and Viola was delighted when any of them dropped by for a visit. Milton bought girl friends home from college to get Mom's approval. Grandchildren showed up for cookies and homemade bread. Daughters-in-law dropped by to chat or perhaps get some of Viola's advice on just about any subject. The family came and went, George A. continued to work in his garden, and Viola continued to nurture them all.

Two marriages took place in those post-war years. On February 13, 1947, Harold married Dorothy in Fort Madison. Brother Milton was the best man, and Dorothy's sister Mildred was the maid of honor. The couple settled in Fort Madison, as had the rest of Harold's older brothers.

Harold and Dorothy Moore
February 13, 1947

George and Viola never owned an automobile and never learned to drive. They spent the greater part of their life in and around Fort Madison, with an occasional trip to Montrose or Keokuk. However, as George invariably implored, they had to be home before the chickens went to roost.

Only once did they journey to Chicago, and that was to attend the wedding of their youngest child. August 14 was the highlight of the summer of 1948 for a number of reasons. Not only did it mark the marriage of Milton and Delores, it required family members who usually balked at leaving Lee County, travel to Chicago, stay in a hotel, and eat in restaurants. For the Moore family, these things were virtually unheard of in those days. To be sure, it was a lavish affair in the eyes of George and Viola. They were gone four days, marking the longest either of them ventured away from home in their entire lives. Nevertheless, it turned out to be a memorable trip and occasion, and they talked for months about their trip to the big city.

Milt and Dee's Wedding
1948

In the late forties, George A. retired from the railroad and settled down to tending his vegetable garden, feeding the chickens, and reading the Evening Democrat newspaper. He had spent more than forty years with the railroad, walking to work every day, seldom missing a day of work, and responding to track problems whenever he was called. It was a well-earned rest for him.

John and Harold, 1950

Despite the addition of a few modern conveniences, arduous work continued for Viola. She still canned fruit and vegetables, washed her clothes in the basement, and hung them outside on a clothesline. She continued to bake her famous cinnamon rolls, tend her geraniums, and read her bible every evening.

Mondays, she would wash clothes in the basement. The Maytag ringer washer and two rinse tubs were an improvement over the washboard and cistern she used in years past, but she still kept the board handy for grass stains or dewberry jam on shirts and pants. Bushel baskets of wrung-out laundry were carried up the basement steps and out the back door to two parallel clotheslines that stretched the length of the yard on either side of the walk. Piece by piece, she would hang the sheets, shirts, and overalls on the line between the freshly tilled soil of George's garden and the brick walkway leading to the chicken house. On each clothesline post, she planted climbing morning glories, mostly purple and pink, that formed an arched floral bouquet over the pathway.

The west side of the house on Avenue I was reserved for the flower garden. Viola favored peonies, asters, and pansies, but her favorites were the roses which climbed a white trellis.

Tuesday was ironing day. The bushel baskets of clothes that had been brought inside the afternoon before were stacked on the sun porch by the ironing board. It was her favorite room. In the autumn, it contained two long tables of slips from her geraniums that she continued to nurture throughout the winter. The morning sun that warmed the linoleum floor, brightened, not only the sun porch, but the adjacent kitchen as well.

Viola May Moore 1949

The sun porch also contained George's wooden desk which had a hinged writing surface and a rusty, seldom-used lock.

Perhaps the item Viola fancied most was the round top Philco radio. It squawked with static but still could be tuned to the soap operas and other programs popular during the forties. "Stella Dallas" and "Portia Faces Life" helped her get through the day of ironing.

She cared for her "adopted" grandson and took a lilac switch to young John on occasion, but probably not as much as was needed. That being said, she loved him as one of her own, and he felt a mother's love for the first time. When Hubert remarried in December 1950, he and John moved away, and George and Viola had their house to themselves for the first time since their newlywed days in Argyle.

Albert and Viola, 1947

Moore/Fowler Outing in Keokuk, Iowa - 1947
Left to Right: Francis and Frances Showalter, Helen Fowler, Hubert Moore, Henry and Hettie Schevers, George Moore, An unidentified man, Viola Moore, John Moore, and Jess Johns.

Sunday visits were the rule in the Moore/Fowler family. Although roads were rough and cars had no air conditioning, a typical Sunday began with church, followed by a drive to Keokuk or to one of the Fowler brother's farms.

The Fowler's, Circa 1948
Albert Fowler, Frank Fowler,
and Arthur Fowler
Clara Fowler, Viola Fowler Moore,
George Moore, Hettie Fowler Schevers

Occasionally, the aging Fowlers would come to Fort Madison, as is shown in this rare photo of the Fowler's together.

Humor played a large role in the lives of the George A. Moores. With eight rambunctious boys, it was a necessary ingredient to balance George and Viola's life of continuous labor. Over the years, Viola collected numerous anecdotes of family antics, and she loved to tell them. She was an exceptional story teller. Some of her favorites went like this:

George R. and Milton

Every year, her boys would collect boards and other materials with which to build a "club house." One of their earlier attempts was not much more than a large packing crate with a few gaps between the boards. Hubert was on the roof nailing on the batten strips, and George was inside to tell him when the nail came through. "Is it through yet?" Hubert would call. "No, not yet," George replied. A few more blows from the hammer and Hubert called out again. "Is it through?" Again, the same reply from George. "It should be through," Hubert chided his younger brother. "Well, it's not," George replied indignantly. With one mighty blow, Hubert hammered the nail well into the board. This time George responded. He had been standing directly under the nail, which had already penetrated a couple of inches past the board's surface. However, it was dark, he was not experienced in nail-watching, and he was looking everywhere except where the nail was being driven. So, brother Hubert had pounded a nail into his brother George's head. Fortunately, it was only a scrape, but Viola would chuckle that perhaps the incident explained a lot about George's behavior in the years to come.

She feigned embarrassment as she told another of her favorite stories. Of course, their home in the 1920's was not modern. The only toilet was in the outhouse at the end of the back walk. One day, a traveling salesman came to the front door and asked to speak to the lady of the house. One of the older boys knew what the situation was and simply said that his mother was not available. However, young Harold piped up, "Yes she is. She's in the toilet." As the salesman turned to leave, Harold ran around the house and saw Viola returning from the privy. He quickly ran back to the front of the house, yelling, "She's coming; she's done."

Stylish Dresses at Milt's graduation from Culver Stockton, 1948

When Roy went to work as a night watchman, his employer gave him a strong search light. Roy brought the light home and was showing it to the family. One of the boys, who Viola believed was Lester, was trying it out by shining it all around from the back stoop. After a few minutes, he directed the light to the alley. The light illuminated a man carrying something which he immediately dropped. Then, he ran. When they investigated further, it turned out that it was their neighbor stealing a large lump of coal. Lester had caught him in the act.

Before Will Fowler died, the Moore family would make the twelve-mile trip to Montrose and visit him at the old home place. There, they would spend hours reliving events of their past and particularly their hunting experiences. When Hubert was a small lad, he wanted to impress his grandfather about his knowledge of wild game. Grandfather Will asked, "Did your brother go hunting today?" Hubert replied, "Oh yes, and we had the game for dinner." "Well, what did you have to eat?" Anxious to please his grandfather, Hubert responded. "We had squirrel, rabbit, and woodchuck pecker."

Will Fowler laughed heartily.

Family Reunion at 1916 Avenue I, 1948
Back Row: Chester, Henry Schevers, George Raymond
Second Row: George Andrew, Donna Jean, Walter
Third Row: Roger, Larry, Barbara Ann
Front Row: John, Russell

Two of the boys decided they wanted to try smoking, so they hid behind the barn. Viola caught them in the act and decided she would teach them a lesson. "So, you boys think that smoking is smart and makes you big men, huh?" she asked rhetorically. "Well, if you want to be big men, you should smoke in public with the men." Then, she made each of them sit on top of a post at the edge of the street and smoke. They smoked and they smoked until they begged to get down. "No, the men from the factory will be along shortly. I think they would like to see just how big you two are." Viola was firm. Eventually, the men began to pass by the Moore house and saw two little boys perched on their posts and looking pretty sick and green, but still puffing away. The laughter of the men and Viola's lesson were both longtime memories for the two smoked-out Moore boys.

Viola's stories included her grandchildren also. She told the story of how Barbara Ann, who was age five, was sent to the store for some eggs. One could do that in those days. In the 1940's, children were safe on the streets of Fort Madison. The little girl was told to bring home half-a-dozen eggs. "That's six eggs," her mother told her. Barbara asked the clerk for six-dozen eggs, an innocent mistake from a five-year-old. The store clerk methodically

The George A. Moore Family
1925
Back Row: Hubert and Roy
Middle Row: Viola, Lester, George Raymond, Chester, and George Andrew
Front Row: Milton, Harold, and Walter

prepared six-dozen eggs and placed them on the counter. Exactly what happened next is unclear, but, after that, Viola never spoke too highly about the common sense of the neighborhood store clerk.

There were literally dozens of similar stories about the Moore family and the experiences they had as they were growing up. Viola knew them all and obtained great enjoyment in telling and retelling the stories long after her boys were out of the nest. The boys and those stories had been her life.

Viola's daughters—in-law were as important to her as were her sons. She used to say that they were the daughters she never had, and then she would look wistfully away because the hurt of losing her only female child at birth would never leave her. Nevertheless, she loved her daughters-in-law, and they loved her. She was Mom to all.

Sundays were meant for family get-togethers. She loved to cook and welcomed any and all who would come by after church for the traditional baked chicken dinner. She plucked the chicken, cleaned it, and put it in the oven to bake. Along with that, she prepared homemade noodles, corn on the cob, green beans, red beets, homemade bread, and two or three pies. George's job was to say grace and finish the meal by saying he only liked two kinds of pie—hot and cold.

Back Row: Delores and Milton
Second Row: Evelyn, Georgia, Dorothy, and Donna Jean
Front Row: John and Larry

Back Row: Hubert, Harold,
Chester, and Lester
Front Row: John

The homestead at 1916 Avenue I was a welcome refuge for any member of the family, whether they had married and were off on their own or not. By the same token, the family pitched in to help make that homestead as livable as possible. One year, four of the brothers heard their father talking about painting the house, and he said he intended to use a broom. They respected the house and loved their mother too much to let that happen, so they brought paint, ladders, elbow grease, genuine paint brushes, and a can-do attitude, and they painted the house from top to bottom in two days. In the process, the brotherly bonds were strengthened and the laughs were many.

The daughters-in-law always brought extra dishes and helped with the serving and the clean up. After the noon meal, which they called dinner, everyone adjourned to the living room or the front porch to "visit." The grandchildren were allowed to go out and play, but, many times, they would stay around to listen to the stories and yarns being told by the adults. It was a truly unique experience.

Dorothy and Harold

George and Viola celebrated their fiftieth wedding anniversary in December, 1953 at their home on 1916 Avenue I in Fort Madison, Iowa. It was a simple occasion, attended by family and friends who had watched them struggle and succeed for five decades.

Viola and George Moore
Fiftieth Wedding Anniversary
December 1953

Life had been tough for the George A. Moores, yet they celebrated the good times, the laughter, and the love that they had interwoven into the fabric of their lives. They lived simple lives, honest lives, and hard working lives, which were bearable because of their faith in God and their love for family. They rejoiced in knowing that the traditions they began, as well as those handed down from their parents, would be carried on by their children and their children's children.

Golden Wedding Anniversary
Back Row: George, Walter, Chester, Hubert, and Harold Moore
Front Row: Viola and George Moore

In 1957, Viola began to feel poorly and eventually had to go to the doctor. After numerous visits, treatments, and medication, Viola was diagnosed with multiple myeloma, a cancer for which, at the time, there was no cure. She died in October, 1957 at the age of seventy.

George A. continued to live at the Avenue I homestead for a few years afterward, but soon he could no longer live on his own. Walter offered to take him in, and his father reluctantly accepted. As the inexorable aging process wore on, eventually George had to be moved to a nursing home, and he lived there until he died in April, 1973 at the age of ninety.

The legacy that they left behind began with the game-hunting Fowlers and the land-tilling Moores, but it has been enriched to be so much more. George A. and Viola Moore, along with the generations before them, have forged a code of conduct for their progeny. Moreover, they imbued in their sons and daughters-in-law a deep sense of family. Brother allied with brother against all others. It was a simple concept, and it worked. It took an unwavering allegiance to family to raise eight boys through all that they faced. They learned and, in turn, passed down traits like a strong work ethic, a humble appearance, a faith in God, and an honest approach to all things. As succeeding generations mature and pass this gauntlet on to the next, the inherited values will pass along as well. The Moore-Fowler history will not be found archived among the great works, but, in its own way, it is nonetheless a story of great people.

PART FOUR:
DESCENDENTS OF GEORGE ANDREW
AND VIOLA MAY MOORE

To tell the individual stories of each of the families that descended from the sons of George and Viola would require volumes. However, it is appropriate to mention them in capsule form.

Roy's Family. The first son, William LeRoy, or Roy as he was called, (1905-1935) married Leona Hoenig (1904-1977) on January 15, 1929. They had two daughters. Lavonne (1930-1994) who married Robert Guthrie Johnson (1930-2005). The younger daughter, Carol June (1932-2004) married Gene Austin Blakley (1929-1984) on August 24, 1950. Roy died of an accidental gunshot wound at the young age of twenty-nine. After several years, Leona married Russell Soland, and they completed raising the two girls.

LaVonne had six children. They are:

Mary Therese Johnson (1953 -) who married William Mcluskey (1950-). They divorced on 4/8/1994. They had two children. Tonya Dene Johnson (1974-) and Bryon Matthew Johnson (1976-). Bryon married Silvia Bausewein (1975-) and they had two children, Tiffany Lynn (1997-) and Megan (2000-).

Ronald Allan Johnson, who died at birth on September 1, 1954.

Larry Michael Johnson (1955-) who married Susan Jolie Foresberg (1959-). They had two children, Paul Jacob (1981-) and Brittany Lee (1986-).

Ann Francis Johnson (1958-) who married Alfred Joseph Pagani (1951-). They had two children, James Joseph (1986-) and Stephanie Ann (1989-).

Ann's twin, Mark LeRoy Johnson (1958-). Mark married Diane Marie Pustejovsky (1958-). They had two children, Kelly Lee (1989-) and Kevin Robert (1992-)

Daniel Robert Johnson (1959-) who married Laura Lynn Randell (1960-). They divorced on 4/15/1997, but had two children, Nicole Danielle Johnson (1990-) and Randall Scott (1991-).

Carol June had eight children. They are:

Patricia Lee (1951-) who married and divorced Steven Clyde Scranton but had two children, Melanie Ann Scranton (1974-) and Leah Diane Scranton (1978-). Patricia

Lee later married Thomas Clyde Nichols and they had a son, Timothy Austin Nichols (1998-).

Deborah Ann (1952-1954)

Gene Austin Blakely, Jr., also known as Rusty (1955-) who married Marjorie Ann Gibney (1960-) and they have five children. Justin Timothy Blakely (1981-1993), Rachael Jean Blakely (1984-), Derrick Anthony Blakely) (1988-), and Shannon Nicole Blakely (1990-). A fifth child, Michele Ann (1978-), was adopted by Rusty. She married Timothy James Saiza (1976-) and they, in turn, had two children, Delesia Cecila Saiza (1997-), and Gavin Martin Saiza (2003-).

Karen Marie Blakely (1956-) who married John Meredith Christ and had three children, Daniel Scott Christ(1984-), Elizabeth Moore Christ (1987-) and John Meredith Christ III (1988-).

Brian Jeffery Blakely (1960-) who married and divorced Sherry King and later married Tammy Sue Cook. They have two children, Brian Jeffery Blakely, Jr. (1985-) and Leah Nicole Blakely (1997-)

Scott Anthony Blakely (1963-) who married and later divorced Tammy Lyn Rippen. They have a daughter, Katherine Ariel Blakely (1992-).

Sandra Kathleen Blakely (1964-) who married Curtis Lee Reeder (1965-). They adopted a daughter from Romania in 1999, Ellise Moore Reeder (1997-).

Leica Ann Blakely (1967-) who married Steve Flores (1967-). They had a daughter, Daisy Blakley (2005-).

Lloyd. The second child of George and Viola was Lloyd Allen (1908-1908), who died in infancy after only three days of life.

Hubert's Family. The third of their children was Hubert Arthur (1909-2005). On June second, 1930, Hubert married Helen Stowe (1911-1991) and they divorced in 1945. On December ninth, 1950, Hubert subsequently married Alma Holterhouse (1908-1984). Early in his first marriage Hubert and Helen adopted a son who they named John LeRoy (1939-) after Hubert's older brother.

John married Sharon Brantley and they had two children. They were Kristen (1964-) and John Anthony (1967-), commonly known as Tony.

Kristen Louise married David Eagleton and they had a son David John Eagleton (1989-). Kristen and David were divorced and she married Thomas Kniest, who had a daughter from a previous marriage, Tabitha (1983-).

John Anthony married Vickie Barker but they divorced. He subsequently married Suzanne Conran. She had a daughter from a previous marriage, Alexa Marie Conran (1990-) John Anthony and Suzanne also had a son, Philip Aidan Moore (2002-).

George Raymond's Family. Next of the Moore children to be born was George Raymond (1911-2001). George married Dorothy Hutchinson (1911-2002). They had a daughter Donna Jean (1935-) who married Dennis O'Laughlin (1932-). Donna had two daughters.

Tara Denise (1961-) married Gilberto Cruz but they subsequently divorced. They had two daughters, Julissa Tara and Caitlin Michelle.

Kelly Jean (1963-), married James Price. Kelly has four children (Gabriel James, Hunter Isaac, Zoe Isabelle and India O'Laughlin.

Chester's Family. One of the twins born to George A. and Viola Moore was Chester, commonly known as Chet. Chester Hiler (1914-2003) married Georgia Sloan (1914-) and they had four sons, Roger (1939-), Russell (1941-), Lloyd (1943-2000), and Glenn (1953-).

Roger married Connie and they had one son, Logan (1973-) who married Sarah Anderson (1973-). They subsequently had a son, Evan (2005-)

Chester Hiler Moore and Georgia Sloan
Wedding Day, December 20, 1936

Russell married Victoria Phillips (1947-) and divorced, but had two children, Eider Brantley (1979-) and Sloan Irene (1985-). Russell subsequently married Diane Hervey.

Lloyd married Igleedtis (Glee) Mitten (1949-) and they had two children. Wendi (1971-) married Marcelo Rodriguez. Dorothy (1973-) married Waylon Sampson and they had a child, Rikki.

Glenn never married.

Lester's Family. Lester Bain (1914-2006) was the other twin. He married Evelyn Watson (1918-2006) and they had a son, Larry (1936-2004). Larry married Sharon (1941-) and they had a daughter, Dana (1964-) and a son, Michael (1966-). Dana married Dane LaFontsee and they have children from Dane's previous marriage. They are Liana (1973-) and Mark Berry (1971-). Michael married Kristen and they have twin sons, Dylan (1999-) and Payton (1999-).

Harold's Family. The sixth child to come along was Harold Lee (1915-). He married Dorothy Kramer (1920-) and they had no children.

Lester Bain Moore and Evelyn Watson
Wedding Day, August 25, 1935

Walter Delbert Moore and Louise Bouls
Wedding Day, June 24, 1940

Velma. Next was Velma Alberta, a daughter who lived but seven days (1918-1918).

Walter's Family. Next to last was Walter Delbert (1921-1981). Walter married Louise Boll (1920-) and they had three children. The first was Barbara Ann (1942-), who married John Perry. They had two children. They are Christina Louise (1962-) and John Jay (1963-).

Christina married Harold Lingenfelter and had three children (Jennifer, Andrea, and Harold III.

Jay married Kimberly Dimlon and they had three children (Evelyn Ann, Taylor Jayne, and Olivia).

Walter and Louise's second child was Mary Louise who died in infancy (1950-1950).

The third child of Walter and Louise was Robert Harold (1951-) who married Karen Cullen (1950-). They had three children (Robert, Andrea and Charlie).

Milton's Family. The tenth and last child born to George and Viola was Milton Earl (1924-). He married Delores Doerfler (1929-) and had two sons and two daughters. They are Milton Scott (1949-), Gary Lee(1950-), Diana Lynn(1957-), and Karen Jeannene(1965-).

Scott married Ann Porter and had three children, (Susan Elizabeth, Carol Christine, and David Scott)

Gary married Jan Stienbecker (1957-) and they have two children (Steve Lumetta by Jan's previous marriage) and Lindsey Marie.

Diana and her partner, Judy Eisenberg, have one child (Lillian Anna).

Karen and her partner Audrey Sakalys have one child (Tyler Anthony).

PART FIVE:
GENERATIONS OF FOWLER'S AND MOORE'S
BY BIRTH AND DEATH DATE

FOWLER

MOORE

Oldest known generation:

John Fowler (/ /1777 - / /18)
Rachel (Roberts) (/ / - / /18)

David Moore (12/7/1764-)
Lucretia (Davis) (8/31/1765-)

Second generation:

John Roberts Fowler, Sr. (/ /1805-11/27/1897)
Harriet (Hammonds) (/ /1808- / /1837)

George C. Moore (12/17/1791-4/14/1873)
Rhoda (Elmore) (12/3/1773-2/14/1868)

Third generation:

William Fowler (9/14/1830-1/16/1921)
Malissa (Bains) Fowler (1/26/1844-2/1/1913)

Shapley Moore (5/10/1829- / /1895)
Melvina (Fickle) Moore(1/5/1841- /1913)

John Roberts Fowler, Jr. (/ /1833- / /1897)
Esther Anna (McChord) Fowler (/ / / /   )

Lucretia (Moore) Pickard (/ / - / /)
Samuel Pickard (/ / - / /)

Edwin Fowler (/ -1835- / /1921)
Emma (Haney) Fowler (/ / - / /)

Leann Moore (/ / - / /)

Fourth generation:

Celestia A. (Lessie) (Fowler) Slater (10/18/1861-4/12/1943)
Terpin Slater (10/8/1856-1/13/1916)

Luella (Fowler) Smith (12/10/1863-3/28/1945)
William Smith (3/15/1864-8/6/1901)

George William Fowler (11/5/1865-6/24/1905)
Elizabeth (Brumagen) Fowler (12/24/1870-3/25/1946)

John W. Fowler (7/28/1868-5/15/1910
Elizabeth (Findeis) Fowler (/ / /-5/27/1942)

James E. Fowler (12/28/1870-4/23/1874)　　　Frank Moore (/ / - / /)

Frank Fowler (9/6/1873-3/29/1963)
Clara (Hagan) Fowler (7/15/1880-10/23/1970)

Mary Hettie (Fowler) Schevers (9/9/1876-4/3/1969)
Henry Schevers (1/7/1876-3/25/1949)　　　Minnie Moore (/ / - / /)

Albert Fowler (2/28/1879-4/3/1968)　　　Chris W. Moore (/ / - / /)
Dora (Sullivan) Fowler 12/25/1880-1/28/1943)

Arthur Fowler (8/28/1881-10/26/1966)　　　Clara Moore (/ / - / /)
Gertie (Dugan) Fowler (3/21/1882-12/20/1952)

Charles Fowler (3/13/1886-3/13/1886)　　　Lula (Moore) Reuther (/ / - / /)

Viola May Fowler (5/22/1887-11/26/1957)　　　George Andrew Moore (7/27/1882-
4/1/1973)

Fifth generation:

Children of Lessie:

Lula (Slater) Swinderman (10/15/1885-8/27/1951)
William Swinderman (4/14/1882-5/20/1969)

Walter Slater (10/15/1890-5/21/1967)
Iva (Ball) Slater (4/16/1894-10/4/1993)

Children of Frank:

Earl Fowler (/ / -10/11/1958)

Mabel (Fowler) Finerty (4/2/1904-9/11/2005)

George Fowler (2/28/1908- / /) *living*

Mildred (Fowler) Deere (8/24/1911- / /) *living*

Marie (Fowler) Lane (8/26/1913-7/25/1991)

Edna (Fowler) Bensinger (8/31/1917- / /) *living*

Children of Hettie:

Francis (Schevers) Showalter (1/31/1926-8/21/2000)
Frances Showalter (9/13/1922-12/9/1995)

Children of Albert:

William Fowler (11/12/1902-3/30/1978)

Elma (Fowler) Frueling (12/22/1904-6/29/2001)
Jesse Frueling (4/20/1896-9/5/1991)

Hazel (Fowler) Anderson (1/16/1907-9/11/1961)
Irwin Anderson (1/7/1902-11/24/1986)

Helen (Fowler) Welden (10/17/1908-10/23/1992)
Glenn Vernon Welden (12/18/1897-12/25/1967)

Wilma (Fowler) Harmon (12/9/1914-4/16/2002)
James Harmon (10/12/1915-11/17/1985)

Children of Arthur:

Hilda (Fowler) Brisby (2/19/1906-11/28/1937)
Allie Brisby (1/23/1901-8/10/1939)

Lloyd Fowler (4/2/1912-8/23/1968)
Ruby (Stockwell) Fowler (12/7/1916-10/13/2001)

Bernice (Fowler) Petty (12/27/1914-8/27/2003)
Glenn Petty (4/21/1913-3/5/1993)

Children of Viola May (Fowler) and George Andrew Moore:

William LeRoy Moore (7/25/1905-5/3/1935)
Leona (Hoenig) Moore (/ /1904- / /1977)

Lloyd Allen Moore (1/25/1908-1/28/1908)

Hubert Arthur Moore (7/03/1909-2/15/2005)
Helen Marie (Stowe) Moore (10/21/1911-3/22/1991) (Divorced from Hubert)
Alma Lenora (Holterhouse) Moore (6/29/1908-11/2/1984)

George Raymond Moore (12/14/1911-9/22/2002)
Dorothy (Hutchinson) Moore (5/28/1915-12/29/2001)

Chester Hiler Moore (3/12/1914-1/21/2003)
Georgia (Sloan) Moore (8/30/1914- / /) *living*

Lester Bain Moore (3/12/1914 -12/2/2006)
Evelyn (Watson) Moore (9/21/1918-4/6/2006)

Harold Lee Moore (10/22/1915- / /) *living*
Dorothy (Kramer) Moore (2/13/1920- / /) *living*

Velma Alberta Moore (11/17/1918-11/24/1918)

Walter Delbert Moore (1/12/1921-5/3/1981)
Zelda Louise (Boll) Moore (2/16/1920- / /) *living*

Milton Earl Moore (4/6/1924- / /) *living*
Delores (Doerfler) Moore (11/21/1929- / /) *living*

Sixth Generation:

Children of William LeRoy Moore

Lavonne Marie (Moore) Johnson (6/8/1930-
Robert Johnson (/ / - / /)

Carol June (Moore) Blakely (1/20/1932-4/18/2004)
Gene Austin Blakely (1/16/1929-2/12/1984)

Children of Hubert A. Moore

John LeRoy Moore (6/28/1939- / /) *living*
Sharon (Brantley) Moore (4/2/1940- / /) *living*

Children of George R. Moore

Donna Jean (Moore) O'Laughlin) (7/31/1934- / /)
Dennis Mark O'Laughlin (12/29/1932- / /)

Children of Chester H. Moore

Roger LeRoy Moore (10/20/1939- / /) *living*
Connie (Chowning) Moore (8/6/1939- / /)

Russell Wayne Moore (5/29/1941- / /) *living*

Lloyd Alan Moore (2/8/1944-7/23/1998)
Igleedtis (aka Glee) (Mitten) Moore (11/26/1950-   / /)

Glenn Earl Moore (9/17/1953- / /) *living*

Children of Lester B. Moore

Larry Bayne Moore (4/25/1936-12/21/2004)
Sharon (Mikulec) Moore (12/11/1941- / /) *living*

Children of Walter D. Moore

Barbara Ann (Moore) Perry (7/23/1942- / /   ) *living*
John Perry (12/18/1942- / /   ) *living*

Robert H. Moore (2/27/1951- / /   ) *living*
Karen (Cullen) Moore (11/5/50- / /   ) *living*

Children of Milton E. Moore

Milton Scott Moore (7/9/1949- / /   ) *living*
Ann (Porter) Moore (12/9/1947- / /   ) *living*

Gary Lee Moore (9/4/1950- / /   ) *living*
Jan (Stienbecker) Moore (4/4/1957- / /   ) *living*

Diana Lynn Moore (7/18/1957- / /   ) *living*
Judy Eisenberg (7/23/   - / /   ) *living*

Karen Jeannene Moore (5/10/1965- / /   ) *living*
Audrey Sakalys (4/24/1964- / /   ) *living*

Seventh Generation:

Children of Lavonne (Moore) Johnson

Mary Therese Johnson (8/1/1953- / /   ) *living*

Ronald Allen Johnson (9/1/1954-9/1/1954)

Larry Michael Johnson (9/21/1955- / /   ) *living*

Mark LeRoy Johnson (2/12/1958- / /   ) *living*

Ann Francis Johnson (2/12/1958- / /   ) *living*

Dan Johnson (/10/1959- / /   ) *living*

Children of Carol June (Moore) Blakely

Patricia Lee (Blakely) Nichols (8/28/1951- / /   ) *living*
Stephen Clyde Scranton (12/13/1949- / /   ) *living* (divorced from Patricia)
Thomas Clyde Nichols (5/14/1960- / /   ) *living*

Deborah Ann Blakely(12/17/1952-2/27/1954)

Gene Austin Blakely, Jr. (Rusty) (3/8/1955- / /   ) *living*
Marjorie Ann (Gibney) Blakely (10/30/1960- / /   ) *living* (divorced from Gene)

Karen Marie (Blakely) Christ (12/7/1956- / /   ) *living*
John Meredith Christ, Jr. (1/18/1959- / /   ) *living*

Brian Jeffery Blakely (2/5/1960- / /   ) *living*
Sherry Lee (King) Blakely (3/16/1963- / /   ) *living* (divorced from Brian)
Tammy Sue (Cook) Blakely (9/2/1965- / /   ) *living*

Scott Anthony Blakely (1/24/1963- / /   ) *living*
Tammy Lyn (Rippen) Blakely (11/29/1962- / /   ) *living* (divorced from Scott)

Sandra Kathleen (Blakely) Reeder (3/20/1964- / /   ) *living*
Curtis Lee Reeder (4/29/1965- / /   ) *living*

Leica Ann (Blakely) Flores (2/28/1967- / /   ) *living*
Steven Finees Flores (5/8/1967

Children of Donna Jean Moore O'Laughlin

Tara Denise (O'Laughlin) Cruz (5/30/1961- / /   ) *living*
Gilberto Cruz (9/23/1957 - / /   ) *living* – divorced from Tara

Kelly Jean (O'Laughlin) Price (3/1/1963- / /   ) *living*
James William Price (8/26/1958- / /   ) *living*

Children of Larry B. Moore

Dana (Moore) Lafontsee (6/2/1964- / /   ) *living*
Dane Lafontsee (11/9/1946- / /   ) *living*

Michael Moore (10/12/1966- / /   ) *living*
Kristen (Giesler) Moore (10/17/1968- / /   ) *living*

Children of John L. Moore

Kristen Louise (Moore) Kniest (3/18/1964- / /   ) *living*
Thomas Kniest (8 29/1962- / /   ) *living*

John Anthony Moore (1/24/1967- / /   ) *living*
Suzanne (Conran) Moore (11/21/1962- / /   ) *living*

Children of Roger L. Moore

Logan Matthew Moore (7/30/1973- / /   ) *living*
Sarah (Anderson) Moore

Children of Russell W. Moore

Eider Brantley Moore (7/12/1979- / /   ) *living*

Sloan Irene Moore (8/8/1985- / /   ) *living*

Children of Lloyd A. Moore

Wendi Caroline (Moore) Rodriguez (2/2/1971- / /   ) *living*
Marcelo Rodriguez

Dorothy Jean (Moore) Sampson (3/4/1973- / /   ) *living*
Waylon Sampson

Children of Barbara A. Moore

Christina (Moore) Lingenfelten (6/03/1962- / /   ) *living*
Harold Lingenfelten (7/22/1959- / /   ) *living*

John Jay Perry (9/26/1963- / /) *living*
Kim (Dimlen) Perry (4/15/1964- / /) *living*

Children of Robert H. Moore

Robert P. Moore (11/21/1974- / /) *living*
Sandra (Kelsow) Moore (3/2/1975- / /) *living*

Andrea M. Moore (8/6/1976- / /) *living*

Charles C. Moore (2/22/1985- / /) *living*

Children of M. Scott Moore

Susan Elizabeth Moore (11/25/1981- / /) *living*
Mitch Kluitenberg (/ / - / /) *living*

Carol Christine (5/7/1985- / /) *living*

David Scott (5/2/1991- / /) *living*

Children of Gary L. Moore

Steve Lumetta (2/4/1978- / /) *living* [stepson]

Lindsey Marie Moore (6/10/1983- / /) *living*

Children of Diana L. Moore

Lillian Anna Eisenberg (1/11/1998- / /) *living*

Children of Karen J. Moore

Tyler Anthony Sakalys (6/19/2000- / /) *living*

Eighth Generation:

Children of Patricia Lee (Blakely) Nichols

Melanie Ann Scranton (12/10/1974- / /) *living*

Leah Diane Scranton (9/12/1978- / /) *living*

Timothy Austin Nichols (2/27/1998- / /) *living*

Children of Gene Austin Blakely, Jr.

Michele Ann (Blakely) Salza (12/18/1978- / /) *living* (adopted from prev. marriage)
Timothy James Salza (5/28/1976- / /) *living* (divorced)

Justin Timothy Blakely (1/2/1981-3/17/1983)

Rachael Jean Blakely (8/7/1984- / /) *living*

Derrick Anthony Blakely (10/28/1988- / /) *living*

Shannon Nicole Blakely (2/3/1990- / /) *living*

Children of Karen Marie (Blakely) Christ

Daniel Scott Christ (7/19/1984- / /) *living*
Elizabeth (Moore) Christ (5/18/1987- / /) *living*

John Meredith Christ III (6/29/1988- / /) *living*

Children of Brian Jeffery Blakely

Brian Jeffery Blakely, Jr. (2/23/1985- / /) *living*

Leah Nicole Blakely (3/17/1997- / /) *living*

Children of Scott Anthony Blakely

Katherine Ariel Blakely (5/15/1992- / /) *living*

Children of Sandra Kathleen (Blakely) Reeder

Ellise Moore Reeder (10/17/1997- / /) *living* (Adopted from Romania in 1999)

Children of Leica Ann (Blakely) Flores

Daisy Blakely Flores (8/7/2005- / /) *living*

Children of Tara Denise (O'Laughlin) Cruz

Julissa Tara Cruz (2/17/1982- / /) *living*

Caitlin Michelle (11/19/1986- / /) *living*

Children of Kelly Jean O'Laughlin Price

Gabriel James Price (10/30/1993- / /) *living*

Hunter Issac Price (1/18/1995- / /) *living*

Zoe Isabelle (10/4/1996- / /) *living*

India O'Laughlin Price (3/17/1998- / /) *living*

Children of Michael Moore

Dylan Moore (7/13/1999- / /) *living*

Payton Moore (7/13/1999- / /) *living*

<u>Children of Dana Moore Lafontsee</u> (from previous marriage of her husband, Dane)

Liana Lafontsee Berry(7/1/1973- / /) *living*
Mark Berry (10/28/1971- / /) *living*

<u>Children of Kristen Moore Kniest</u>

Tabitha Ann Kniest (6/19/1983- / /) *living* (From previous marriage)

David John Eagleton (11/26/1988- / /) *living*

<u>Children of John A. Moore</u>

Alexa Nicole Conran (9/5/1990- / /) *living* (From previous marriage)

Philip Aidan Moore (6/21/2001- / /) *living*

<u>Children of Wendi C. (Moore)Rodriquez</u>

Mateo Lloyd Rodriguez (/ 2 /2006

<u>Children of Dorothy J. (Moore) Samjeson</u>

Rikki Samjeson (9/8/1991- / /) *living*

Alexi Samjeson (5/8/2002- / /) *living*

<u>Children of Logan M. Moore</u>

Evan Matthew Moore (6/22/2005- / /) *living*

<u>Children of Christina (Moore) Lingenfelten</u>

Jennifer (Lingenfelten) Mellinger(9/2/1983- / /) *living*

Devin Mellinger

Andrea Lingenfelten (2/16/1985- / /) *living*

Harold Lingenfelten III (4/1/1989- / /) *living*

Children of John Jay Perry

Evelyn Perry (7/17/1991- / /) *living*

Taylor Perry (12/20/1992- / /) *living*

Olivia Perry (9/21/1994- / /) *living*

Children of Robert P. Moore

Ryleigh Moore (7/31/2002- / /) *living*

Robert H.. Moore (4/5/2004- / /) *living*

Children of Susan Moore

Alyson Kaitlyn Moran (5/24/2001- / /) *living*
(Adopted by John and Karen Moran)

Ninth Generation:

Children of Michele Ann (Blakely) Salza

Delesia Cecilla Salza (7/25/1997- / /) *living*

Gavin Martin Salza (7/25/2003- / /) *living*

Children of Julissa T. Cruz

Lina Isabel Julissa Duke (3/7/2001- / /) *living*

Jasmine Olivia Duke (3/24/2004- / /) *living*

Ninth Generation (Continued):

Ninth Generation (Continued):

Ninth Generation (Continued):

www.ingramcontent.com/pod-product-compliance
Lightning Source LLC
Chambersburg PA
CBHW052008280526
45793CB00005B/897